Think Like a Scientist

WRITE LIKE A SCIENTIST

Philip Wolny

Britannica
Educational Publishing

IN ASSOCIATION WITH

ROSEN
EDUCATIONAL SERVICES

Published in 2019 by Britannica Educational Publishing (a trademark of Encyclopædia Britannica, Inc.) in association with The Rosen Publishing Group, Inc.
29 East 21st Street, New York, NY 10010

Distributed exclusively by Rosen Publishing.
To see additional Britannica Educational Publishing titles, go to rosenpublishing.com.

First Edition

Britannica Educational Publishing
J.E. Luebering: Executive Director, Core Editorial
Mary Rose McCudden: Editor, Britannica Student Encyclopedia

Rosen Publishing
Amelie von Zumbusch: Editor
Nelson Sá: Art Director
Brian Garvey: Series Designer
Tahara Anderson: Book Layout
Cindy Reiman: Photography Manager
Karen Huang: Photo Researcher

Library of Congress Cataloging-in-Publication Data

Names: Wolny, Philip, author.
Title: Write like a scientist / Philip Wolny.
Description: New York : Britannica Educational Publishing, in Association with Rosen Educational Services, 2019. | Series: Think like a scientist |
Audience: Grades 3–6. | Includes bibliographical references and index.
Identifiers: LCCN 2017059660| ISBN 9781538302347 (library bound) | ISBN 9781538302354 (pbk.) | ISBN 9781538302361 (6 pack)
Subjects: LCSH: Science—Methodology—Juvenile literature. | Technical writing—Juvenile literature.
Classification: LCC T11 .W6527 2019 | DDC 507.2—dc23
LC record available at https://lccn.loc.gov/2017059660

Manufactured in the United States of America

Photo credits: Cover, p. 1 kali9/E+/Getty Images; cover (top), back cover, interior pages background cetus/Shutterstock.com; pp. 4, 15 © AP Images; pp. 6, 13 © Encyclopædia Britannica, Inc; p. 7 Universal Images Group/Getty Images; p. 9 Andy Cross/Denver Post/Getty Images; p. 10 Carlton Ward/NATIONAL GEOGRAPHIC IMAGE COLLECTION/Getty Images; p. 12 tdoes/Fotolia; pp. 16, 17, 18, 28 Hero Images/Getty Images; p. 19 Portra/DigitalVision/Getty Images; p. 21 lightpoet/Shutterstock.com; p. 23 haryigit/Shutterstock.com; p. 24 Dino Osmic/Shutterstock.com; p. 26 antoniodiaz/Shutterstock.com; p. 27 Sergei Kozak/Corbis/Getty Images.

CONTENTS

CHAPTER 1

THE SCIENTIFIC METHOD

Scientists ask questions. We sometimes call that scientific inquiry. Scientists often inquire about problems they want to solve. For any problem, they try to understand a cause so they can come up with a solution. By learning what causes a disease, for example, scientists can work to control its spread. Then they might try to cure it!

These geologists are taking water readings while doing fieldwork. Geologists study Earth's physical features and history.

The process that scientists use to solve problems is called the scientific method. They find out as much as possible about something. Then they make a **hypothesis**, an attempt to explain the problem. They test the hypothesis with an experiment. Then they collect and analyze the results, or the data. If the experiment does not support the hypothesis, the scientists think about the problem again and develop a new hypothesis. They then test that

THINK ABOUT IT

How is a scientific problem different from a problem you might have at home or school?

VOCABULARY

A **hypothesis** is an attempt to solve or explain a scientific problem.

hypothesis with a new experiment. If the experiment supports the hypothesis, other scientists repeat the experiment to make sure that they get the same results. If they do get the same results, the hypothesis will be accepted as true until it can be proven false.

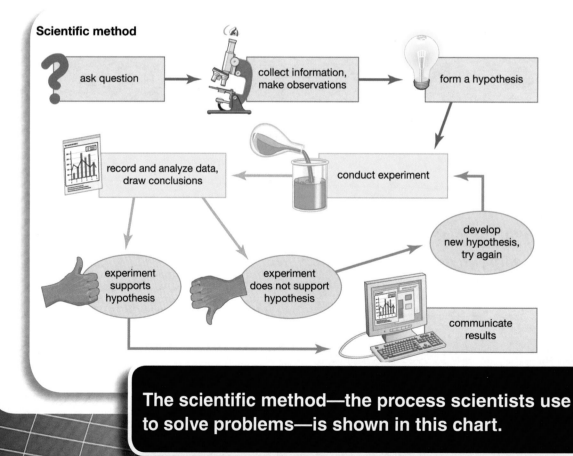

Scientific method

ask question → collect information, make observations → form a hypothesis

record and analyze data, draw conclusions ← conduct experiment

experiment supports hypothesis

experiment does not support hypothesis

develop new hypothesis, try again

communicate results

The scientific method—the process scientists use to solve problems—is shown in this chart.

One part of science that many people do not think about is writing. A good scientist must know how to express his or her ideas well. In addition, many of the different sciences have their own specialized vocabulary and rules for explaining things. This is true for physics, chemistry, geology, and many others. Part of scientific inquiry is learning these vocabularies and using them in writing.

Nicolaus Copernicus wrote a book explaining his theory that Earth and the other known planets circle the sun. The book was published in 1543.

CHAPTER 2

THINKING LIKE A SCIENTIST

Scientific experiments depend on exact results. Scientists need to be clear in everything they do. This is true whether they work on an unproven hypothesis or double-check a well-known theory. Being clear helps everyone else understand their work. Sometimes, a scientist must communicate to others in the same field. Other times, a biologist might develop ideas that chemists or physicists could learn from. Sometimes scientists want to communicate with nonscientists like you and me about important discoveries in their fields. When scientists are clear and use the right scientific language, they can make sure others will benefit and learn from their work.

Some words mean slightly different things to scientists than they do to nonscientists. We might hear the word "observation" and think about something interesting we noticed the other day—for example, "All cats are cute." A scientist's observation is more precise. It is the act of gathering information by noting facts or occurences. It involves looking at and describing something in detail. The scientist then uses that detail to figure out how certain things work.

A researcher tags a tranquilized bear in Florida. What questions do you think a scientist might have about bear behavior?

Scientists also think about the world in a certain way. In scientific inquiry they begin by identifying a problem. This is not an everyday problem you may have ("I have too much homework" or "I can't find my favorite song on You-Tube"). Rather, it means a question about why things are how they are.

THINK ABOUT IT

Why is it important for scientists to make detailed observations?

For example, imagine wondering where the moon came from. The problem or question might be phrased as "How did the moon develop or come into being?" Once they have a question, scientists make observations to try to answer that question. Scientists sometimes use special words to explain their findings or hypotheses. For example, to answer the question about the moon, scientists in the 1800s developed the **fission** hypothesis: A very long time ago, they said, Earth was spinning so fast that a piece of it split off and flew into space, ending up as the moon.

VOCABULARY

Fission is a splitting or breaking into parts.

Much later, astronomers developed new hypotheses. These were based on newer evidence and described more likely reasons behind the moon's creation. One of them was called the giant-impact hypothesis: billions of years ago, a large object slammed into Earth. A big part of Earth broke off and became our moon.

The word "theory" also means something different to scientists than to nonscientists. A scientific theory is an explanation for why things work or how things happen. Scientists come up with theories based on their observations and the

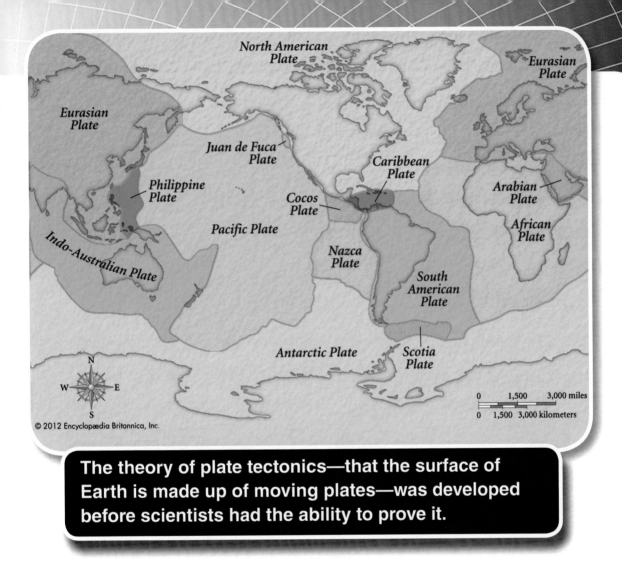

The theory of plate tectonics—that the surface of Earth is made up of moving plates—was developed before scientists had the ability to prove it.

evidence they find. They make hypotheses and do experiments to test their theories. Theories are not based on a guess.

CHAPTER 3

WRITING LIKE A SCIENTIST

There are some rules for science writing that are accepted in most or all areas of science. Others differ among different **disciplines**.

Whatever kind of scientist you might be, you want your readers to understand what you are saying. Consider this sentence: "The evidence presented by me proves the cheese was eaten by the mouse." And then this one: "My evidence proves that the mouse ate the cheese." Which

VOCABULARY

Disciplines are specific subsets of a larger field. For example, physics and biology are disciplines of science.

This scientist is examining the fossil of a flying dinosaur. The discipline he specializes in is paleontology, the study of things that lived millions of years ago.

one do you understand better and faster? They are both saying the same thing, right? But the first one is much longer. It also uses the passive voice, which is when something is acted on by something else ("the cheese was eaten by the mouse"). The second sentence is shorter and more direct. It uses the active voice, which means that the subject acts upon something else ("the mouse ate the cheese"). In general, it's better to use the active voice. That way your reader can keep straight who is doing the action. It also lets you say what you want to say in fewer words.

Another part of writing to think about is verb tense. In writing about an experiment you performed, you might use past tense to describe the steps of the experiment: "First, I placed some cheese on the floor. Then I watched and waited at a safe distance with my notebook and my camera." The conclusion will probably use some present-tense wording, however. For instance,

What tense would you use to describe the steps of an experiment you did last week? What tense would you use in the notes you take during the experiment?

THINK ABOUT IT

What verb tense do you use when telling someone about an argument you had? What verb tense do you use to describe your feelings about it?

"Based on the results, I conclude that mice like to eat cheese."

Using active voice and the proper tense are important in any kind of writing. Scientists need to keep those in mind, but they also need to know how to write a scientific report. All scientific reports follow a set order and include the same sections. Sometimes the sections can be combined or called something different, but they should all have the same basic information. A report for your school's science fair should be a simpler version of a paper by a famous scientist.

Here is a breakdown of what a scientific report should include:

- **Title:** This should tell readers specific information about the experiment.
- **Abstract:** This is a general statement about the experiment. It is a summary of the information in the rest of the report.
- **Introduction:** In this section you should explain why you performed the experiment. It should include the question that you wanted to test and the hypothesis. It should also mention what you already know about the subject.

Scientists write scientific reports and articles to share the results of their work. They read others' reports to learn about the latest discoveries.

- **Materials and methods:** This section lists all of the equipment and other materials that you used. It also tells how you carried out the experiment. That includes how you gathered data and how you recorded that data. It should provide all the information needed for someone else to carry out the same experiment in the same way.
- **Results:** The results are what you learned in the experiment. This section should list the data that you gathered and all of the observations that you made. It can include tables, charts, and graphs as well as written explanations.
- **Discussion/conclusion:** This part of the paper explains the results. This is where you will decide if your hypothesis was proved or not. Here you will discuss whether the data that you gathered answers your original question in a way that can be proved or not.

- **Reference list:** This section should list the sources—books, articles, other science experiments—used to help set up and write about this experiment.
- **Appendices:** An appendix or appendices (more than one appendix) may be added to the end. This is a place to show all of the data you collected, other charts or tables, or any other information that would be useful to readers to understand or appreciate your experiment.

CHAPTER 4

WRITING UP AN EXPERIMENT

Now that you know the general rules for writing about an experiment, let's look at an example. For instance, let's imagine an experiment about testing different batteries made by groups in a classroom. Students can make batteries from many different things. These can include food, like potatoes and lemons, and wires and other parts made of different metals. Teams A, B, and C build their own batteries and see how much power each can create.

Here is how you might write your report about the experiment:

- **Title:** Comparing Materials in Creating Improvised Batteries.

Here you can see how a battery powered by several lemons can provide enough electricity to make a light bulb glow.

- **Abstract:** This experiment tested batteries made out of different materials. Some materials worked better than others at providing power for a light bulb.

- **Introduction:** We know that different materials can be used to make simple batteries. We wanted to see whether a potato, a tomato, or a lemon worked best. Our hypothesis was that they will all work the same.

- **Materials and methods:** We used potatoes, lemons, and tomatoes. We also used a small store-bought battery as a control variable. We used four voltmeters, four small light bulbs, wires, and nails. We connected the wires and light bulbs to the potatoes, lemons, and tomatoes. We also connected a voltmeter to each and read the meter to see how much power each battery produced.

· **Results:** The batteries made by teams A and B, using the tomato and the lemon,

Digital multimeters, such as the one hooked up to this lemon, measure voltage as well as electrical resistance and current.